Emotions

No fear of negative feelings

The twelve pure feelings

Feelings, emotions and mood

Serenity

The feeling of rage and its manifestations

Recognize and understand emotions

I.Theory of emotions

1. Direction and intensity of the emotional motion

2.Theoretical distinction, and the nature of emotions

3.Elements of Greek and Roman rhetoric to influence the   emotions

4. Functions of emotion

II. Theory of cognitive psychology

Emotions, and their influence on phenomena, symbolization and aesthetic perceptions

To find book and e-book list, go to HUBERTUS IHN under Amazon Kindle

No fear of negative feelings

Negative emotions as shadow the positive feelings that drive us through life and determine our decisions and our well-being. Cut a glade (Propose a free space) in the forest of consciousness, Heidegger.

Positive emotions tend to have a feel-good character. Negative emotions have a more warning character.

We believe our logical mind shows us the right path through life. From time to time – especially with (central) crucial and difficult decisions – we have doubts whether the path we want to pursue is the right one. We come to the brood. We are ruminating. We go through the alternatives, weigh the advantages and disadvantages and are unsure whether alternative the chosen by our logic thinking is the best. We use phrases/concepts such as: the glass is half full or half empty. With an optimistic or a pessimistic view, or believe that we are supposedly making a realistic decision.

The one or the other is trying to feel out with his guts or with his feelings if the decision is correct. Just follow your heart and your feelings! What do I love, towards what do I have an affection, what would give me joy/pleasure/ delight ? With what was I successful ? With what did I fail?

In everyday life, we use the terms "affection" or "dislike" aversion , or what do I find likeable or dislikable/unappealing sympathetic or unsympathetic. These processes often occur unconsciously and within seconds. Rarely, these processes step up to the reflexive consciousness.

Outward signs, such as clothing, appearance, body language, facial expressions, tone of voice, etc. influence our evaluations /assessments of likeable or dislikable/unappealing or affection or aversion.

Even with these mixed feelings lying on the surface subconscious processes are happening / taking place . If you drill down deeper, one can say with Levi Strauss: "I feel like a road junction where things are happening, I just do not know why?"

Deep Low-lying pure feelings, such as love and hate, grief, joy or anxiety escape our consciousness due to by taboo or lack of experience

They manifest represent themselves through

dreams or - in clairvoyance through images and are usually not consciously accessible.

We want to feel good, positive and happy! Sadness, anxiety, rage, fury, ire, wrath, bad temper, are socially not accepted, they disturb our well-being and are displaced (pushed to the side) . But they do tell us that something is wrong. They do not reach our consciousness and we cannot make use of these feelings.

We fall into depressive, manic and obsessive conditions, at worst into psychoses and neuroses. Dissatisfaction, hectic and shortage of time are spreading. We think this is normal because our environment is expecting this and behaves in the same way. (Standardized feelings).

We try to regain our center with relaxation

techniques, meditation, entertainment, consumption, etc. Nevertheless, there remains a musty, lifeless and unsatisfied feeling so that we are trying to cover it up. We hope that things will get better or that our children will do better. We accept it, also because others are feeling the same way. Life is not a rose garden, and if so then at least with thorns. But is it really so?

How do our perception channels determine our feelings and conversely, how do our feelings determine our perception channels?

Which direction / orientation do we have in terms of visual, auditory and tactile haptic senses ? What type we are? Which channels are we mainly using? Do we dislike the smell of something ? Can we not smell that? Did we dislike the taste of something ? Something did not like us?   Through these questions and those words we use, we can get closer to our deeper feelings. Then something happens emotionally.

The three monkeys: hear nothing, see nothing, feel nothing are the opposite. The first step towards schizophrenia and alienation.

Can we get closer to our deeper, pure feelings by consciously switching on and off of our perception channels approaching - but also to our negative feelings?

Which emotions are playing a crucial big role in everyday life? Rather positive ones - or rather negative ones?

In terms of emotions: What type am I ?   The amicable and loving type, the bold or rather (anxious), melancholic and suspicious person?

The twelve pure feelings:

Positive - Negative

Love - Hate

Joy — Sadness

Courage - Anxiety

(painless) Wellbeing - Pain

Serenity – Fury (rage)

Pleasure - Suffering

(See Hubertus Ihn, Theory of Emotions, Amazon, Kindle, 2013)

These twelve pure feelings as well as the

mixed emotions, such as anger, compulsion, restlessness, depression, manic emotions etc. unconsciously control our thoughts and behavior.

We think and we act logically, weigh the pros and cons.

But our compulsions, anxieties, hopes and impulses take command.
According to Professor Seligmann - former chairman of the American Psychological Association - happiness research and positive thinking should show us the way.

The Greek word for happiness is eudaimonia. If we translate it directly from the Greek, it means to have a good access to the mediators between the spiritual world and the people. The syllable "Eu" means well. The syllable "daimonia" (demons) means -

directly translated from ancient Greek - an intermediary between the higher world and man.

The mediator between man and the "higher world" are the feelings.

If I have made the right decision, then I feel good, I am not afraid, I am neither depressed, nor sad or angry.

I'm satisfied, happy and enjoy my life.

Myself , up to the age of 30, suffered from manic depression. Either I was totally psyched up and funny. I was invited to every party as an entertainer. Or I did not see anyone and depression took hold of me.

I could not detect any feelings either in myself or in others. I had no words or terms for feelings or emotions. I have never taken any medication for that. The feeling of fear was unknown to me. I could not recognize human emotions neither with myself nor with others.

Already the ancient Greeks had a word for this phenomenon. They called people like me "Alogothymicians". You have probably never heard of this word. Neither had I.

The Greek word "thymus" means feeling or emotion (Latin).

The word "Logo" means the word.

"A" means zero or not.

An Alogothymician" is a person who does not know any words for feelings or emotions.

I think that all of you can recognize emotions in others, though maybe not all of them and not all of the time. It will depend on the strength of the feelings of the other person.

Do you recognize your own feelings?

Are you aware of them?

Are you aware of what moves you?

Can you recognize how your feelings affect your thoughts, your behavior and your actions?

Most likely you do, especially when your emotions are very strong But a lot remains hidden to you.

You are buying something. You are going to work. You are watching TV and are listening to music. You make conversation and you are doing sports.

Are you satisfied with that?

Do you feel good?

You are enjoying your life and live in a wonderful world!

Don't you want to keep your world?

Do you think that this world of yours might not be good or may be threatened?

You are happy and satisfied - and this will stay so?

Don't such thoughts creep up ?

And if such thoughts do creep up, are you dominated by them?

You are not watching any thrillers, political talk shows, fantasy movies, political documentaries, sports reports and horror news? You are not buying insurance and are accumulating money?

Well, if so, then anxieties and compulsions do not matter to you.

But if they play a role in your life, then you should think about your behavior!

How often do you think about negative things and how often do you think about positive things?

Do you have pleasant conversations or do you rather discuss serious issues?

Or is it rather small talk about something trivial, such as sports, the weather or what you have just done or what you are going to do?

Do you rather turn to pleasant things or do you rather dwell on problems and unpleasant things that happened to you?

Are your topics related to the past or to the future? If so, then your thoughts are not dealing with the present. Not with things which could bring you joy. Although future or past topics can also be pleasant.

Feelings, emotions and mood (temper)

In this context should be distinguished feeling, emotion and mood (temper?). In the German language, the words feelings and emotions mean the same thing, both in everyday language as well as psychologically. Conceptually, the word emotion and the word feeling must be distinguished. When I say the sentence: "I have the feeling" it is clear that I feel something. This "feeling" can relate to the perception of emotions coming from outside and as well to internal emotional condition. Which emotions are present in the environment or with other people? Or what emotional condition do I have inside?

With the feeling I can trace both the internal or external emotions.   Emotion (Latin) means " to come out from the state of rest". The basic condition of emotion or feeling is peace and quiet. When the feeling comes out from the state of rest, the emotions appear. Anger, joy, mourning, anxiety, cold rage etc.

In the Greek language, the words "feeling" and "mood" translate as "thymus". Similar to how we have to distinguish conceptually between feelings and emotions it is also necessary to distinguish conceptually between feeling and mood (temper).

The word "mood" relates to the basic condition of the flexibility of feeling, while the word "emotion" designates the specification - as for example anger, joy, mourning, anxiety, rage etc.. states and types of mood (temper)

Mood (temper) is derived from courage. Coziness (German Gemütlichkeit) means comfort. Plato's Phaedros distinguishes the soul into mood (thymus) and impulse (drive).

Adjectives for the mood: Sunny, simple, cheerful, childlike, gentle, sensitive. Heated temper, ruin my mood, depress someone.

To be added are: Irritable, phlegmatic, quiet and energetic, stable mood (temper) (see also: Clausewitz below), very agile, little lively, emotionally immobile.

Clausewitz: The strong mood will not get out of balance.

4 mood types according to Clausewitz (see Wikipedia.):

Little lively: Phlegmatic

Very lively, very agile: people whose feelings never exceed a certain level – empathetic, calm people

Very irritable: Emotions ignite quickly and violently like gun powder (dynamite) , but are not of permanent nature.

The feelings are slow moving, can reach great strength and are of permanent nature. These persons have energetically deep rooting hidden passions (Emotional character).

In the science of psychopathology, people with rapidly changing emotional conditions (states) are referred to as "borderline syndrome".

Serenity

In the spectrum of the twelve pure feelings serenity is defined as the opposite of the word "rage". In the Greek language, serenity is called "ataraxia" which directly translates as "not restless", therefore meaning rest (silence).

The condition of silence is the basic state of the feeling, meaning that there is no emotion moving out of the state of rest. The state of rest can certainly be felt, however , it is not an emotion in the sense of "moving out".

After much deliberation and discussion, I have come to the conclusion that serenity not only means rest (silence), but it also includes the "let be" or "let go".

If something is not moving (at rest),

nevertheless moves, so this seems to be a contradiction at first.

When the moving out from the state of rest cannot be pressed into an emotional form, a pure feeling, such as rage, anxiety, joy, love, mourning, etc., but is swinging loosely through the spectrum of feelings, meaning that the emotion is let loose with regard to its vibrations, then we call this "serenity".

On the one hand, serenity can be compared to the "hardly perceptible smile of the Buddha", on the other hand the vibrations of the feelings can be described with exuberant, happy, funny, lively, rising mood and creative .

The opposite of rage is serenity, i.e. certainly a condition of "let go of something". Not to be affected by something, but to ignore it untouched. This will make an enraged person even more furious.

Possibly irritate him.

This can be observed very well with children who are usually closer to their feelings than adults. A child can change quickly from a state of rage into a joyful, cheerful or enthusiastic mood. The rage is quickly forgotten. The child is happy again. The opposite from cheerfulness to rage is also possible.

In summary, the opposite of rage is the lively, cheerful and harmonious serenity.

If the condition of the lively, cheerful and harmonious serenity stabilizes as a character trait, this can be described as a state of mood. In the categorization of Kretschmar that is called "sanguine".

The opposite is the choleric, furious character structure or state of mind.

In this context, there is still to be mentioned the sad, melancholic, phlegmatic character structure with a depressive tendency.

Phlegmatic can be viewed as slowed down, choleric as explosive and sanguine as cheerful and elated mood.

The serenity can manifest in adults in various forms.

The cheerful upbeat (elated) serenity

The clouded and darkened serenity (In music minor)

The serious, unconsciously hidden feelings (Externally serene personality)

The deliberately controlled and hidden feelings (diplomatic behavior, coolness). The acting and only outwardly serene personality.

The word "Persona" translated from Latin means mask. The two latter forms mentioned above are to be regarded as masked emotional states of serenity.

It is somewhat complicated. The four forms of serenity can all occur in a masked form. However, there is a difference.

The cheerful and clouded serenity does allow feelings. A person is working with his feelings and shows them to the outside. This process requires energy. This is the repertoire of the actor.

The consciously or unconsciously hidden serenity does also require energy for its suppression. However, it is less energy intensive.

Note: In my opinion, the masking of the mood by the public people as well as the actors can be regarded as one cause for the increased consumption of drugs.

The constantly distorted emotional states of mood and masking of the mood drive a person out of his own center, overwhelm him and go along with high energy consumption. In order to find the center again, to recharge quickly and to keep up the masking, drugs are taken.

The feeling of Rage and its manifestations

Much like hate, joy and mourning, the word

"rage" cannot be found with the German version of Google. They mention such words as for example "Wutbürger " (a new German word meaning rage citizen). Also Wikipedia does not go into great detail.

Going back to the Old Germanic language, rage (German : Wut) can be associated with "god Wotan". Wuotan - the raging. (in German: der Wütende).

The rage is associated with the feelings of aggression, anger, wrath and fury (which means - translated from Italian - as frenzied applause or attracting high attention).

Rage is taken personal, while wrath and ire evolve over something.

While wrath and ire are rather notionally related emotions, rage and fury are pure emotions that are not or only slightly connected with thoughts.

This can best be illustrated in the context of love. One can distinguish three kinds of love:

Making love or sexual love.

The spiritual or platonic love, based on similarities of the thoughts and interests (Mental love).

The pure emotional love: Father's love, kids love, love for a friend, love of the world, etc.

The mental rage is called wrath or ire, and anger is certainly also of mental, emotional nature.

The physical rage, like physical love, can certainly best be characterized by: she was red with rage or he was pale with rage or the cold rage. A red or pale face can be a sign of rage.   A pale face can also be connected with the feeling of anxiety. A red face also displays shame or excitement. The strong emotions of rage have a physical effect on the circulatory system. The blood rushes into a person's face due to the excitation, in case of a pale face, the blood disappears from his face. A kind of numbness or shock stops the blood from flowing.

The physical rage manifests itself frequently by yelling, clenched fists, strong physical movements like beating and kicking.

If the rage remains hidden – by conscious or unconscious control - it is visible externally only by a slightly indicated furious facial expression or body posture, or so well hidden that the suppressed rage is not visible. Should the person be able , whether consciously or unconsciously, to suppress the rage so that no physical reaction is visible or internally encroaches the body, it is the pure rage.

Recognize and understand emotions

I.Theory of emotions

1. Direction and intensity of the emotional motion

2.Theoretical distinction, and the nature of emotions

3.Elements of Greek and Roman rhetoric to influence the   emotions

4. Functions of emotion

II. Theory of cognitive psychology

Emotions, and their influence on phenomena, symbolization and aesthetic perceptions

1. Basics of symbolization and perception and the truth

2. The process of symbolizing phenomena

3. Dimensions of aesthetic knowledge and Kants aesthetic perception

4. Conclusion

5. Literature

Recognize and understand emotions

You are dealing with psychology? Here is a little story to the words of the psyche!

The "soul". Derived from the old Germanic language the word "soul" means: The one coming out of the water.

In the German language the word "soul" means "Seele".   The syllable "See" means "water", and the syllable "le" means "coming".

Psyche: derived from ancient Greek, means the core of the grain. The stuff corn flour french baguettes are made out of.

The corn /grain which may be lying in the desert for centuries: When rain falls on it

– new life, a new plant grows out of it, it' s create.

The psychology deals with the feelings. The Latin word for feelings is emotions.

We think that our thoughts, our logic leads us.

But subconsciously, we are guided by our emotions or feelings.

I.Theory of emotions

1. Direction and intensity of the emotional motion

There are two bipolar direction of emotion. Colloquially, we distinguish:

Positive bad, evil or good-negative, benign

In these two directions of motion, there are twelve bipolar expressions of pure feeling you could also name as categories of emotion or feelings.

Positive - Negative

Love   - Hate

Joy   - Sadness

Courage – Anxiety, Scarring?, German Angst

malaise, - Pain
painless ?

Serenity - Rage

Lust ?   - Suffer

The "?" above mean: I ask myself, is lust a pure feeling and if so what feeling is its contrast? Pain? Think about it. We can keep talking. I believe lust and suffering. This begs the question: "Are lust and suffering, pure feelings?"

Furthermore, there are two states of emotion.

Tranquility - restlessness (movement)

In Latin we call tranquility as concilliare. restlessness or motion is referred to as movere (Latin). The emotion is thus the removal moving to moving out from the rest, E means out. Movere (Latin) referres to that which is moved.

Now, this emotion has two properties for the time being. Firstly, the movement, on the other hand, notion (colouring) of the movement. If the movement is very strong as well as the respective distinct feeling is very strong. So the person feels strong love, intense anxiety or sadness on the other hand, if the movement is not as strong little love, little sadness, low anger is felt. Notion (colouring) of movement reverres to the way of expressing the twelve bipolar expressions of pure feeling , e.g. hate, love, sadness.

For most people it is not possible to extract pure emotions so to become conscious of it. Most people are aware of the idea of linguistic content sitting on their feelings. Though they spot the underlying feelings only in a reduced form. The emotions can trigger physical reactions . Often you notice these feelings only on others but not on yourself.
Feelings you can easily perceive on yourself e.g. anxiety causes a sinking feeling in my stomach, some people are pale with fear, cold sweat, increased heart activity.

Anger can be accompanied by physical reactions following: A red head, gesturing strong, loud voice, piercing eyes, distorted facial expression, etc.

Most people are aware of more mental, verbal and physical expressions in others or themselves. Their reactions are especially linguistically or physically. Rarely sadness, fear or anger is perceived directly, even more rarely do people react by conscious emotions.

2. Theoretical distinction, and the nature of emotions

Psyche or soul as we may designate the whole of life, or life energy from organic especially human existence. Whether it is that the soul of us is entered from the outside of some parent and possibly go back again escapes. Be it that of the molecular structure of the organic to the unicellular this life that distinguishes organic from inorganic arises.

The emotions are a part of the psyche or soul, and are regarded as the side part and expression of the soul. In German, these emotions are called feelings.

In its pure form, it is possible for the emotions to swing. They swing between love and hate, e.g. or between joy and sorrow to and fro. They can also be changed, that is Pain, love, anger, sadness, etc. can take over or control the body and mind, and thus of the entire individual at certain times.

The capability to vibrate and the exchange of emotions suggest that the nature of the source of emotions energetic nature (generally known of as vital energy) and, among many other properties can be oscillatory.

Similar to an electric, magnetic or gravitational a field of feeling or emotion can exist.

Most people have little influence on the emotions and are often dominated by them. Good rhetoricians and priests are able to influence other people through language, voice, melody and color (pathos) of their speech.

3. Elements of Greek and Roman rhetoric to influence the emotions

The three elements of Greek rhetoric:

Ethos (target of the speech)

Pathos (passion by the choice of location feeling cheerful, sad, hateful, and the volume and speed of language affects the strength of emotion or excitement.

Pragma (The content, the structure, the reasoning, etc.)

The three elements of Roman rhetoric:

Movere: moving the masses and soldiers to use them for the imperial power of Rome

Concilliare: So that they calm the masses and soldiers gather strength and energy to fight

Docere: The art of lecturing, the content, the structure of the argument, etc.)

The difference between the Roman to Greek rhetoric consists essentially in the fact that the Greek is emotionally nuanced. More details later. Similarly to today's rhetoric, the visual component is crucial. (See Sammy Molcho)

Furthermore there are several ways to influence emotions by light and temperature of a room.

4. Functions of emotion

In addition to the energy field and oscillating character, the emotions can have the following functions:

Mediation between body and mind (consciousness)

Mediation of feelings within collectives or groups (common shared joy or mourn)

Control and selection of channels of perception as eye, ear, etc. (knowledge selection, stimulus selection)

Control and selection of thought (consciousness)

Control of the action as it is intuitive, instinctive and intellectual respect of the preconscious

In summary, one can say that emotions can have directing, mediating, vibrating or pulsating character.

5. Literature

Gadamer, H. G.: Die Aktualität der Schönen. Reclam, Stuttgart 1977, gedruckt 1998

Linster, H. W.: Gesprächspsychotherapie. In:

Linster, H. W., Wetzel, H. (Herausgeber)
Veränderung und Entwicklung der Person:
Grenzen und Möglichkeiten psychologischer
Therapie. Hoffmann und Campe, Hamburg
1980 S. 170-129

Rogers, C. R.: Die klientenzentrierte
Gesprächspsychotherapie. Kindler, München
1976

Hubertus Ihn: In Theorie der Psychologie;
Theorie der Emotionen, 2013, Amazon
Kindle, Smashword

Hubertus Ihn: Theorie der kognitiven
Psychologie unter Berücksichtigung der
Phänomenologie, 2013 Amazon Kindle,
Smashword

II. Theory of cognitive psychology

Emotions, and their influence on phenomena , symbolization and aesthetic

perceptions

1 Basics symbolizing and perception and truth

Truth of a model in mind is the image of reality and thus usually a subjective part of the truth .

The process of becoming aware of the advantages or unconscious done by Symbolize (see Gadamer, pp. 29, Chapter 41 2S , . Rogers, 1976, p 438) .

Symbol is a Greek word translated into englisch , it is called memory shard . A host give the guest one half of a broken shard , the other half of the shard he keeps for himself. Comes after years someone with the shard again and he holds them together, in this way he can be recognized by the host. It can be regarded as antique passport matters . (Gadamer , p 41)

The symbol is thus the anker can be

perceived with . The symbol can be a word ,
sound, taste , smell, touch, image or
emotional feeling . (Corresponding to the six
channels of perception) .

The six channels of perception

Vision (eye)

Hearing (ear)

Taste (mouth, tongue)

Smell (nose)

Keys (skin)

Feel (? , Waves? Field ?)

As long as something is not symbolized , the
event or the object escapes the consciousness
of the viewer .

Each psychodiagnostic process should begin
to determine what feelings the client

expresses, he can recognize the feelings and concepts with which he occupied this . Rogers referred to the evidence of the feelings with words as symbolization . To symbolize in this context as well means becomming conscious. Many are unconscious emotions in many people. The concept of awareness and practice is a key element of psychotherapy. A repeatedly highlighted problem of psychotherapy is the defense of awareness of feelings in the form of blocks, transmissions , etc.

2. The process of phenomena symbolization

If you translate the word phenomenon in the German language , it means appearance . Colloquially, the word phenomenon is viewed as appearance of an object , a person , an event , etc. . In the sense that man is a phenomenon . The moon or the sun appears . Furthermore, the sun is shining.

But the term phenomenon also has a second meaning , namely in the sense : That seems to me to be wrong or that appears dark or light, long or short , etc. to me.

From this example it is clear that the appearance of a hand can come from an object on the other hand takes place as a reflection of reality in consciousness. The representation of reality in consciousness is referred to as a phenomenon (appearance) ..

Especially people living creatures take the reality is not objective and is usually not completely equally true. This awareness creates a model of the observed reality and every viewer has mostly a different model than the next . See Heidegger and Husserl.

There are three levels of analysis :

The objective reality or the appearance of reality

The model of the objective reality or the appearance in consciousness , the phenomenon (symbol)

The reaction behavior or feelings about the model of the objective reality

3. Dimensions of aesthetic knowledge and aesthetic perception of Kant

How the various phenomena (phenomena) are created in the minds of the viewer? Helps us here by Kant defined aesthetic knowledge further . A better formulation than aesthetic knowledge is aesthetic perception .

For many , the term aesthetics from the Greek means translated into German , beautiful. How they will admit a very subjective matter . However, already in ancient Greece , the word has aesthetically beautiful addition to the significance and the importance of sensory perception . Sensory perception is fundamentally different from the logical / empirical perception.

The logical / empirical perception often defines general rules for an objectified , abstract model is based.

The aesthetic and sensory perception is influenced by Kant, by means of two fundamental dimensions :

Through the six channels of perception

Vision (eye)

Hearing (ear)

Taste (mouth, tongue)

Smell (nose)

Keys (skin)

Feel (? , Waves? Field ?)

By the selected , perceived characteristics of the observed reality

For example:

beautiful ugly

Scented smelly

pleasantly uncomfortable

bitter sweet

light dark

loud low

Trist stimulating

The symbols or anchor in consciousness known as phenomena linked according to the used channels of perception , images (eye) , sounds (ear) , taste (tongue) , feel (? , Wave? Field ?), Etc. and the perceived characteristics such as light, dark , tall, short , etc. , the perceptions of the idea .

Phenomena are therefore symbols of perception caused by the currently selected channels of perception and perceived , observed properties of the reality or the objects. Phenomena are so often subjective and varied.

Six channels of perception and hundreds, if not thousands, of properties in different people create 100 thousands if not millions of different images of reality or phenomena. Even a man can have any number of phenomena in consciousness , depending on which channels it uses perception and considers the properties of the object it .

Unused channels of perception relevant or relevant characteristics of reality or even the denial of reality , lead to the distortion of the same , re-interpretation and misinterpretation . Incorrect symbols and phenomena lead us astray . We do not perceive components of reality , no symbols are formed in consciousness. The reality is unconsciously in terms of Freudian conception. Note: in particular, their own feelings are symbolized usually a small extent. This has , as we shall see later catastrophic individual, social and political implications.

The relationships described above are to be regarded as selectivity of the channels of perception and reality properties

4. Conclusion

Faith, hope, feelings are mixed (category two) and are assigned to the courage .. Sympathy in the sense of affection, recognition is attributable to the pure feeling of love.

In contrast to the pure feelings of the mixed emotions associated with physical sensations and mental ideas .. Trust, hope and sympathy are particularly connected in the above connection with thought. In-depth version of the mixed feelings (category two) will be published in a separate article .

Outshine current feelings and emotions of the character , usually unconsciously aesthetic awareness dimension, shall add a third dimension , the feelings , the symbols. They formation phenomenon and determine that most unconsciously .

The aesthetic and sensory perception is characterized by three dimensions :

Through the six channels of perception

By the selected , perceived characteristics of the observed reality

In much of the current feelings and the character structure

The own emotional state is often interpreted into reality and thus forms the model of reality in the light of this present state of feeling from . The timid character structure of a person reinforces this interpretation. A man will be ängstligender the darkness or a dark cellar as terrifying perceive. The courageous man is the dark cellar perceive but not be frightened . A person who has had bad experiences in the dark , will look at the dark basement as threatening as a man who has had any bad experiences in the dark.

Note: Fear is assigned to the term anxiety and mixed feelings .

Literature

Gadamer , HG : The timeliness of beauty. Reclam , Stuttgart , 1977, printed 1998

Linster , H. W. : psychotherapy . In : Linster , HW, Wetzel, H. (Eds.) Change and development of the person : limits and possibilities of psychological therapy. Hoffmann and Campe , Hamburg 1980 pp. 170-129

Rogers , CR : The client-centered psychotherapy. Kindler , Munich 1976

Hubertus Ihn: In Theorie der Psychologie; Theorie der Emotionen, 2013, Amazon Kindle, Smashword

Hubertus Ihn: Theorie der kognitiven Psychologie unter Berücksichtigung der Phänomenologie, 2013 Amazon Kindle, Smashword

To find e-book list, Hubertus Ihn under
Amazon Kindle – Books

Emotion Control

Theory of emotions

Next to find e-book list, Hubertus Ihn under
Amazon Kindle - Books

Anthology feelings

Other E-books:

Mourning

Anxiety

Rage

Pleasure

Theory of cognition

Theory of consciousness

www.ingramcontent.com/pod-product-compliance
Lightning Source LLC
Chambersburg PA
CBHW070823290526
45795CB00002B/821